SECRETS OF

BOOK

Document Number One in the Public Record
Office of Britain's National Archives – that is the
proud position of the Domesday Book, the survey of his new realm
ordered by William the Conqueror in 1085. A county-by-county
record with no parallel in Europe, Domesday's pages have been
pored over first by administrators, later by historians. By Victorian
times, Domesday had become a national treasure. Imbued with
mythic status, its name known to millions who have never read a
word of it, Domesday is one of the most remarkable documents ever
compiled – and the story of how it was made is just as remarkable.

ABOVE: *Great Domesday's entry for Clungunford (Clone), Shropshire. The Domesday Book had 44 lines
to the page, with headings in red ink. To make place names stand out, a red line was put through them.*

Domesday Now and Then

*'He sent his men all over England ... and had
them find out ... what or how much everybody
had who was occupying land in England, in land
or cattle, and how much money it was worth.'*

During the Christmas holidays at Gloucester in
1085, William the Conqueror revealed his big
idea. For the past 20 years, he had been King
of England. His Norman army had stamped its steely
control over the land since winning the Battle of
Hastings in 1066, when the Saxon King Harold lost
his life and his lords their lands. Now it was time to
set down, in black and white, how things stood in
the England that belonged to William.

The result was the ultimate tax survey, telling the
king how much revenue he should be getting. It was
also the record that counted in any legal disputes.
Who was entitled to which bit of land? The survey
held the answer and its decision was final. Nobody
was exempt, and argument was pointless, just as it
would be on Doomsday – the final Day of Judgement
by Almighty God.

This was why the English wryly called the survey
'Domesday', a name first recorded around 1179 when
Richard FitzNeal, treasurer to King Henry II, wrote:
'There are several things in the vaults of the Treasury,
which are taken about the country, and are locked up
... such as the king's seal ..., Domesday Book, the
roll of demands ...'.

The questioning of landholders and tenants was
completed quickly, within a year, but the royal scribes
had not finished writing the final version when
William died in September 1087 and work stopped.
There were two volumes – Little Domesday, holding
the raw results from Essex, Norfolk and Suffolk; and

ABOVE: *Fountains Abbey in Yorkshire, a 12th-century Cistercian foundation. Its immense size and wealth testified to
England's monastic energy in the post-Conquest period.*

LEFT: *The Bayeux Tapestry depicts the appearance of Halley's comet. Possibly dismayed by such an omen, King Harold fought bravely but lost the Battle of Hastings and his life. His lands passed to the victorious William.*

Great Domesday – so-called because its pages are bigger than Little Domesday's – giving the edited, shortened summary of information from all the other English counties (except Northumberland and Durham) and a small part of Wales. Some counties yielded little; only a few places in Cumbria are mentioned, for example. There is no coverage of Winchester, where Great Domesday was probably written, or of London. It has been suggested that Winchester, seat of the king's Treasury, may have been a tax-free zone, while two blank pages in the Middlesex section were possibly intended for London's entry.

ABOVE: *Hugo the Illuminator, a self-portrait of a scribe sketched in a manuscript margin around 1110.*

ABOVE: *Mounted Normans, swords aloft, drive English foot-soldiers from the field at Hastings, where hacked bodies testify to the ferocity of their onslaught.*

Who wrote the Book?

Great Domesday seems to have been completed by a single English scribe, able to handwrite an amazing 3,500 words a day. A second man then made corrections. He was French, and may also have been in charge of the whole survey. Some have suggested he was Samson, William I's chaplain and later Bishop of Winchester. Another candidate is Ranulf Flambard, who became chief finance minister to William II (Rufus). Several scribes helped to write Little Domesday.

Reading Domesday

'And the land was troubled with many calamities arising from the gathering of the royal taxes.'

Domesday is easy to read – but not always to understand. Written in Latin, with many short forms and abbreviations, its world is strange to us, featuring ranks in society and jobs that no longer exist, measurements no longer used and place names (often Latin versions of English) that may have changed out of all recognition since it was written. But, decoded, Domesday Book lifts the lid on life in England 900 years ago.

William's survey split the country into seven areas, each visited by three or four royal commissioners. One, Bishop Remigius of Lincoln, toured the Worcester circuit with his assistants, questioning both rich and poor at the county courts. Answers were required (but do not always appear) in triplicate. People had to declare the value of their holding: '… as it was in the time of King Edward, as it was when King William gave it and as it is now.' Replies were edited and entered, county by county, in Great Domesday.

ABOVE: *Stokesay in Shropshire was held by Roger de Lacy, whose father Walter, the guardian of William's borders with Wales, died the year before Domesday.*

First there was a list of the county's main towns and landholders; then came a description of its estates (manors), starting with the king's. Church estates came next, followed by the lands of barons, knights and ordinary people. This pecking order mirrors Norman England's feudal society. Sole landowner was the king, the winner of England in battle. He let land (fiefs) to his chief warriors (barons) in return for military service. Barons leased land to knights and knights to farmers and villagers, who owed various duties and payments in return. At the bottom of the heap were slaves.

Domesday shows that free peasants were most heavily clustered in the old Viking area of eastern England – the Danelaw – though numbers had fallen sharply over the country since 1066, and their social status had dropped. Most peasants in Norman England were not free, however, but tied to the manor where they were born. Of highest rank were the villagers (villeins) who worked their lord's land as well as the farm plots they rented from him. Smallholders (bordars) had less land, while cottagers (cottars) cultivated a patch of ground near their home. Slaves, most numerous in the south and west, made up around a tenth of the population, but – perhaps surprisingly – were fewer in number than before the Conquest.

RIGHT: *A peasant with a scythe muses mournfully on changing times. At harvest time, some peasants had to reap their lord's crop in August. Others had to provide three days' labour a week.*

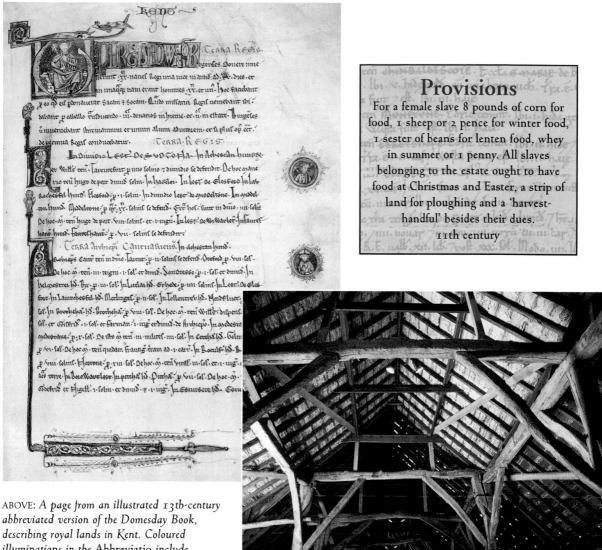

Provisions

For a female slave 8 pounds of corn for food, 1 sheep or 2 pence for winter food, 1 sester of beans for lenten food, whey in summer or 1 penny. All slaves belonging to the estate ought to have food at Christmas and Easter, a strip of land for ploughing and a 'harvest-handful' besides their dues.

11th century

ABOVE: *A page from an illustrated 13th-century abbreviated version of the Domesday Book, describing royal lands in Kent. Coloured illuminations in the Abbreviatio include pictures of the king (enthroned at the top), archbishops, bishops and barons.*

ABOVE: *The timber roof of Abbot's Hall Barn, now at the Stowmarket Museum of East Anglian Life. Crops collected as tithes were stored in barns all over England, under the supervision of the local reeves.*

ABOVE: *Shepherds and sheep in a pre-Conquest Saxon painting. Sheep were important to the livestock economy and Domesday records high numbers – 1,000 at Mildenhall in Suffolk and 1,600 at Puddletown in Dorset, for example.*

Domesday Village

'To this manor has been added ½ virgate of land; it has been concealed
so that the King has had no tax from it …'

Eastleigh, Devon

ABOVE: *Domesday extract for Eastleigh (Lei), in Devon,
The abbreviation TRE stands for tempora regis Eduardis —
'in the time of King Edward' (the Confessor), while the
entry's last line notes 'and the king has had no tax from it'.*

Most people in Norman England lived in the country, on the manor of a wealthy noble or churchman who might hold several far-flung estates elsewhere. At Domesday, the king held around 17 per cent of the land; bishops and abbots 26 per cent; with 54 per cent shared by around 190 other tenants-in-chief. A dozen barons held a quarter of England.

Land was measured in hides (or carucates in Viking areas), roughly 60–120 acres, which was reckoned to be what an eight-oxen team could plough. Recording the number of ploughs a manor owned, Domesday reveals that farmers in fertile Sussex worked more than four plough teams per square mile. Hides could be split into four virgates; carucates into eight bovates; sulungs, yokes and leets were other local names. County shires were split into hundreds, or wapentakes in Viking areas.

Domesday assessed what a manor was worth to its lord each year in money (taxes) and kind (crops, animals, etc.) from his peasants. Dues from a mill or a mine on his land, the number of pigs kept, eels caught and so on all had to be included. Estimates put the land's total value at around £73,000 a year.

RIGHT: *Sheep graze where Domesday peasants ploughed and planted their strips of land, known variously as lands, flats, intakes and selions. Furrows, still visible, were made by ox-ploughs. On heavy soils, the furrows helped drainage.*

RIGHT: *Royal forests had been set aside for royal hunting since Anglo-Saxon times. William's New Forest in Hampshire is mentioned in Domesday, along with 35 'parks for wild beasts' and other enclosed areas into which game was driven.*

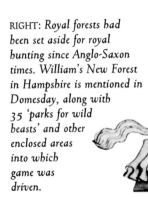

'In Kettering are 10 hides for the king's geld [tax]. And of these 10 hides 40 villeins hold 40 virgates ... and all the men render 50 hens and 640 eggs. And besides this, Ailric holds 13 acres with 2 acres of meadow, and pays for them 16 pence. And there is a mill with a miller and it pays 20 shillings. And 8 cottars ... and they work [for the lord] 1 day each week and twice a year they make malt. And each of them gives 1 penny for a he-goat if he has one and 1 halfpenny for a nanny-goat.'

'In Collingham there are 4 carucates and 1 bovate less a fifth part of 1 bovate for the king's geld ... And there are 20 villeins who hold 1½ carucates. Each one of these works for the lord throughout the year 1 day in each week ... And all these men bring 60 cartloads of wood to the lord's court, and ... dig and provide 20 cartload of turves, or 20 cartloads of thatch. And they must harrow throughout the winter. And each year they pay 4 pounds of rent.'

Isle of Ely

'The Isle is ... most delightful for charming fields and pastures ... remarkable for beasts of chase ... fertile in flocks and herds. Its woods and vineyards are not worthy of equal praise. There is an abundance of domestic cattles and ... wild animals; stags, roes, goats and hares ... a fair sufficiency of otters, weasels and polecats .... In the eddies at the sluices ... are netted innumerable eels, large water-voles, with pickerels, perches, roaches, burbots, and lampreys, which we call water-snakes ... There you will find geese, teal, coots, didappers, water-crowns, herons and ducks, more than a man can number.'
Description by a French knight to William I, c.1070

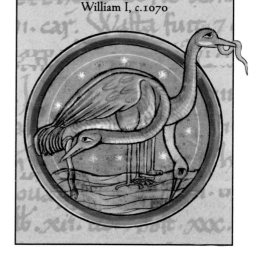

ABOVE: *A medieval goatherd. Many Domesday farmers kept goats for milk, rather than cows. Castle Hedingham in Essex had 100 goats recorded, together with 160 sheep and 100 pigs.*

ABOVE: *Hawking, shown here in an English manuscript illustration c.1030, was also popular with the Norman conquerors. Some Domesday communities were required to produce a hawk in lieu of tax money.*

Domesday Farming

Farming was already intensive, with a quarter of all land managed as pasture or meadowland for grazing livestock. Riverside meadows also produced hay (worth 10 shillings a year profit in Oxfordshire). Sheep were plentiful, besides cows, oxen and horses. Goats (over 4,000 in Suffolk) supplied milk; prized pigs rooted for acorns and beech nuts among woodland trees coppiced for timber. Around 15 per cent of England was covered by woodland.

ABOVE: *Fish, drawn to illustrate the constellation Pisces in an 11th-century manuscript. River fishing rights were usually reserved for the landholder.*

Crops of wheat, barley, oats and beans grew in around 35 per cent of England's soil. People milled grain by hand, or took it to one of Domesday's 6,000 watermills (windmills took another century to appear). Mills could be money-spinners, for the miller took a cut from every customer. But when crops failed, people went hungry; 1086 was a '… toilsome and sorrowful year … through murrain [plague] of cattle … corn and fruits were at a stand …'.

Among goods rendered on rent day was honey, the only sweetener available; but 'if anyone [in the county of Herefordshire] has concealed a sester [about 32 ounces] of honey … and this is proved, he pays five sesters for the one'. Religious observance of meatless Fridays meant fresh fish on the menu instead, often including – on Domesday evidence – eels from millponds and weirs. The Isle of Ely in Cambridgeshire teemed with them (so gaining its name) and the yearly haul of 27,150 eels from Doddington, Cambridgeshire, included many destined for the Abbot of Ely's table. The Abbot, a big landholder, had no liking for his new Norman rulers. He called Picot, Sheriff of Cambridge, 'a roving wolf, a crafty fox, a greedy hog, a shameless dog …'.

Rents were payable to the steward who ran the manor, directing the farm bailiff who hired workmen such as carpenters and smiths. The yearly round of ploughing, harrowing, sowing and harvesting was organized by the reeve, who might be elected as spokesman by the peasants. Business was conducted at the lord's hall, which served as a courthouse of justice as well as a home.

ABOVE: *A medieval watermill, with eel traps set in the mill-race. Eels – a popular, nourishing food in Domesday times – might also form part of the rent. Some lords of the manor claimed every second fish caught at the weir.*

ABOVE: *Peasants using wooden spades tipped by an iron shoe, fashioned on the farm by the estate blacksmith.*

ABOVE: *Saxon farmers thresh and winnow corn, from an 11th-century calendar. Wheat, barley and oats were the common crops. Villeins had to leave their own work if the reeve needed help on the lord's land.*

ABOVE: *Bees and their hives, from a medieval manuscript. Blakeney in Norfolk had to supply a night's honey and 100 shillings in customary dues, while Methwold had 27 hives.*

RIGHT: *Farm animals, like this frisky cow, were usually left to forage for themselves. A lord might send for all the village cattle to graze on his fallow- or grass-land if he needed extra manure for his soil.*

Estate rights and customs

'A cow-herd ought to have an old cow's milk for a week after she has newly carved …. A shepherd … should have 12 nights' dung at Christmas, and 1 lamb from the year's young ones, 1 bell-wether's fleece … and bowl-full of whey or buttermilk all summer … Every tree blown down … ought to go to the woodward.'

11th century

9

Domesday Masters and Mistresses

Most Domesday landholders were men, and big estates were almost all in northern-French hands. Holding more land than anyone but the king was William's half-brother, Robert, Count of Mortain. Land passed to Norman control from Englishmen like Arni, of Neston in Cheshire. Once a proud landholder in his own right ('he was a free man'), in Domesday he appears as an under-tenant to William FitzNigel, a Norman. Again, 'Miles Crispin holds Wootton [Bassett, in Wiltshire] from the king. Leofnoth held it before 1066.' But Thorkill of Arden was the English exception. By cooperating with Duke William, he managed to hold on to the Warwickshire land of his fathers.

Domesday's few women are mainly, but not exclusively, great ladies. 'Queen Edith [Edward the Confessor's wife and King Harold's sister] held it [Selborne, Hampshire]. It never paid tax. The king gave ½ hide of this manor with the church to Radfred the priest. Value before 1066 and later 12s 6d; now 8s 4d.' Two other landholder queens were William's wife Matilda, who died

ABOVE: *Robert, Count of Mortain, half-brother of the Conqueror, fought alongside him at Hastings and gained the reward of more land in England than anyone but the king.*

in 1083, and the wife of King Harold (or Earl Harold, as Domesday calls him, denying his right to the Crown).

One Domesday noblewoman, the pious Lady Godiva, rode into legend – bareback and naked – through the streets of Coventry, campaigning to reduce the tax burden imposed on its citizens by her husband Earl Leofric. Although she was dead by the time of Domesday, Godiva's holdings in Leicestershire, Nottinghamshire and Warwickshire had not yet been re-assigned.

A very different countess was Judith, niece of William I, who proved loyally Norman by betraying her rebel husband, Earl Waltheof, to the king. Waltheof, last of the English earls, was duly executed (reportedly reciting the Lord's Prayer, which his severed head finished off loud and clear). Judith's reward was to receive more land from the king. Further down the social scale, a girl named Aelfgeth held land from Godric, Sheriff of Trent, as a reward for teaching his daughter the graceful art of gold embroidery.

ABOVE: *The Domesday entry for Selesburne (modern Selborne in Hampshire) shows it as a royal manor, formerly held by the English Queen Edith. A tax-free haven, it passed to William at the Conquest.*

ABOVE: *Noble ladies enjoyed the thrill of the chase, hunting and hawking even when they were (to modern eyes) unsuitably dressed.*

LEFT: *This illustration from the Bodleian Library's Caedmon Genesis manuscript (Anglo-Saxon poetry on Old Testament subjects) usefully portrays what the fashionable English lady wore.*

LEFT: *Brave but bashful, Lady Godiva on horseback. This 19th-century statue, sculpted by John Thomas, recreates the naked ride through Coventry that sought to relieve its citizens' tax problems.*

Snippets of daily life

Humbler women are not always named. In Gloucestershire, 'Walter's wife gave a manor of 5 hides to St Paul's for her husband's soul ...', while from Worcestershire, 'Wulfin who lay ailing made sure that his friends and priest heard his wish that his wife should hold his land for as long as she lived ...'. From Norfolk come two 'true life stories': 'On Alwin's death, King William gave his wife and land [in Norfolk] to Richard, a young man.' And 'A man of Wihenoc's loved a certain woman on that land, and took her as his wife ...'.

Domesday Religion

'The church at Kettering belongs to the altar of Peterborough. And for the love of St Peter it renders 4 rams and 2 cows or 5 shillings.'

The Norman Church was a ship of state as well as a saver of souls. Bishops were often as powerful as earls and William's own half-brother, Odo of Bayeux, was one of England's great landholders, with estates in 22 counties. The Church, a bulwark of royal power, provided much of the manpower for the Domesday survey, from scribes to commissioners such as William, Bishop of Durham, who held lands in nine counties.

William expected the Church to render its dues. Only six years after the Conquest, he ordered the Abbot of Evesham to instruct 'all those who are subject to your administration' to produce 'all the knights they owe me, duly equipped'. Evesham Abbey itself was expected to send five knights for military service, and it was the Abbot's job to find them.

Abbots grew very powerful. Domesday records that the freemen of Long Melford in Suffolk 'could not ever grant or sell their lands without the Abbot's full consent'. That Abbot was Baldwin of St Edmunds (where pilgrims travelled to visit the shrine of the martyred King Edmund). The abbey had two mills and two fishponds, 118 monks, 30 priests, deacons and clerks, 28 'nuns and poor persons', 75 bakers, ale brewers, tailors, washerwomen, shoemakers, robemakers, porters and cooks – and 34 knights. Baldwin, who had been Edward the Confessor's doctor, held lands in seven counties.

ABOVE: *Lines from the Domesday Book reveal that the Abbot of Thorney in Huntingdonshire caused the loss of 300 acres of grazing land.*

ABOVE *Bishop Odo of Bayeux, the Conqueror's half-brother, deputized for him in England while William was in Normandy. He became Earl of Kent, but was imprisoned at the time of the Domesday survey.*

The priest was, with the reeve, the foremost resident of a Domesday village, and although a thousand or so priests are mentioned in the survey, there were undoubtedly many more. Nor are all the parish churches listed. Some priests had good livings, receiving a tithe (tenth) payment in goods or money from the people they served. But the poorest lived as other villagers, doing manual labour. Many priests were married, despite recent laws introduced by the Normans against clerical marriage, and some had inherited the post from their fathers.

Claiming that the English Church was corrupt, in 1070 William had imprisoned the Archbishop of Canterbury, Stigand, seen by the Normans as covetous and worldly. He was replaced by the gifted Italian, Lanfranc (c.1005–89), who set about 'reforming' the English Church, bringing it closer to the practices of the mother Church of Rome and putting Norman abbots in charge of English monasteries. The only English bishop to remain in his see was the saintly Wulfstan of Worcester.

LEFT: *The tithe barn at Great Snoring (Snaringa), in Norfolk. More than 2,000 such barns were built in England between 1066 and 1400.*

RIGHT: *A monk receives a tonsure from a fellow brother. The Roman tonsure used in Norman times involved shaving a circular area on the crown of the head, sometimes leaving a fringe to symbolize Christ's crown of thorns.*

ABOVE: *The nave of Durham Cathedral. This mighty building was begun in 1093, after Benedictine monks imported by William had replaced the old Anglo-Saxon monastic community, of which St Cuthbert (d.687) had been a member.*

Domesday Towns and Traders

Towns were tiny in Domesday England; only 18 had over 2,000 citizens but around 100 are recorded as the home of 'burgesses' (inhabitants of a borough, with special privileges). Towns fostered trade and industry, ensuring that some, like Oxford (243 dwellings) and York (800 houses), would grow during the later Middle Ages, while others – such as Thetford in Norfolk and Dunwich in Suffolk – sank into obscurity.

Close-packed towns of wooden houses with straw thatch meant that fire was a constant hazard. Allowing fire to spread resulted in a fine, plus compensation to neighbours for any damage. A man accused of setting fire to a house had to produce 40 witnesses to prove his innocence. The king was eager to profit from death by natural causes, too, through death duties – '… if a stranger lived and had a house in Oxford, and died there, the king had whatever he left'.

Norwich, boasting 421 burgesses, had grown rich on wool – Domesday records that the city had '2,100 sheep – and one goshawk'. Other towns were centres of local trades that still continue – as, for example, ironworking at Corby, Northamptonshire. Iron mines also occur in the entry for Rhuddlan (Cheshire), while Gloucester supplied iron from the Forest of Dean for the king's ships. Derbyshire was the country's sole supplier of lead, from mines worked at Wirksworth and Matlock Bridge.

ABOVE: *A Norman at work. Most large roofs in England were made of oak. Abbeys or churches needed three or four roofs to span the whole building, the middle roof resting on pillars and arches that divided the interior.*

A key industry was the production of salt, needed to preserve meat and fish, and Droitwich (Worcestershire) had more than 260 salt-pans. Other salt towns included Nantwich in Cheshire, but the industry here seems to have been declining. The new Norman Earl of Chester, Hugh Lupus ('Hugh the Fat') found only one salt-pan still working. Domesday records that the industry was worth only one third of its pre-Conquest value.

Town markets were important assets but subject, like retail outlets today, to downturns from unwelcome or unfair competition. The entry for Thetford records that '… in this manor there used to be a market on Saturdays. But William Malet [a Norman] made his castle at Eye, and he made another market … and thereby the Bishop's market has been so far spoilt that it is of little value …'.

Markets were regulated to try and prevent illegal trading, with appropriate fines imposed on miscreants: '… anyone giving false measure was fined 4d … making bad beer meant punishment with the dung stool …' [Huntingdonshire].

ABOVE: *Lines from Domesday Book relating to the fines for overloaded salt carriers in Cheshire (see opposite).*

LEFT: *English place names such as Saltings, Budleigh Salterton and Seasalter remind us of the ancient salt-making trade. This illustration from a 15th-century Dutch manuscript shows brine being boiled to crystallize the salt.*

Paying for salt

Anyone who 'purchased salt in a cart' from the salt towns of Middlewich and Northwich [Cheshire] paid 4d in toll if he had four or more oxen; if he only had two oxen, he paid 2d. 'Anyone who so loaded his cart that the axle broke ... paid 2 shillings ...; who so loaded a horse as to break its back also paid 2 shillings ...'.

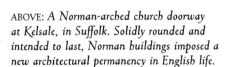

ABOVE: *A Norman-arched church doorway at Kelsale, in Suffolk. Solidly rounded and intended to last, Norman buildings imposed a new architectural permanency in English life.*

BELOW: *A shipwright at work. Wooden ships from east-coast ports sailed across to Scandinavia with cargoes of corn, cheese and salted beef, returning with fish, furs and timber, as well as hawks for English falconers.*

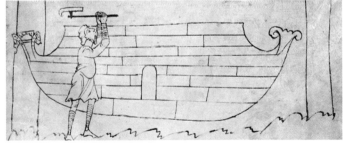

LEFT: *Saxons warming themselves while working at the smithy. Iron-working was an important Domesday occupation, but with fire a constant hazard there were many penalties for carelessness.*

Domesday Country

Domesday shows a changing England. The old English nobility had been swept away – killed in battle, driven into exile, or dispossessed of their lands. But change affected every level of society. Before 1066 people had often paid rent in kind (the people of Bakewell, Ashford and Hope in Derbyshire paid in honey and five cartloads of lead, as well as coins), whereas after the Conquest cash payment became more common. The survey also shows clearly the impact of the Norman Conquest on land values. In northern England, values fell by about a quarter between 1066 and 1086 – testament perhaps to William's savage campaigns of destruction to subdue the north.

We can recapture only part of the picture of England in 1086. Many place names listed in Domesday are unfamiliar – having changed with the passage of time, or vanished from history. The survey lists only heads of households, and records are scanty for people living in castles or monasteries. Most estimates of England's population put it at between 1¼ and 2 million – below the 4 to 5 million of

ABOVE: *A sturdy Welsh spearman. Not easily subdued, the Welsh maintained a prickly presence along the border with England, confronting William's Marcher barons and their 'radmen' (riders) and 'rad-knights', mentioned in Domesday.*

Roman times. Lincolnshire, East Anglia and eastern Kent seem to have had the most dense populations (10 people per square mile), three times the figure for northern England. Dartmoor and the Welsh Marches were also thinly populated, with fewer than three people per square mile.

But hidden in the survey's short, pithy entries are odd facts that paint fascinating details of life just after the Conquest. Vineyards, measured by the arpent (about an acre), were cultivated in Domesday England, abundantly in Middlesex. Women landholders might be called a lord's 'man' (homo), in the sense of owing duties and obligations to a lord. Lords living in the Welsh border counties needed a number of 'riders' and 'riding-men' to act as 'minders' or outrider escorts. Landholders from across the Channel were emphatically distinguished as 'Frenchmen' in some entries. In the same way, Domesday's words may tell us how history has treated the people who appear in its pages. 'Villein' and 'boor' – respectable English peasants – degenerated in meaning, perhaps as a result of how they were viewed by their Norman rulers.

ABOVE: *King Harold rides with hawk and hounds through pre-Domesday countryside. Note the Saxons' luxuriant moustaches – most Normans shaved their top lips.*

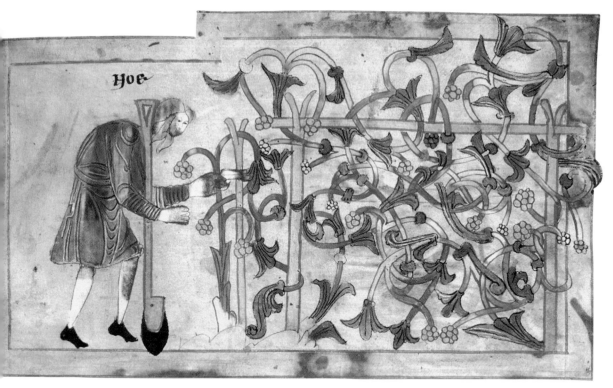

HOE

Civitas de Leorcestre Tépore Regis Edwardi, reddet p annú regi .xxx. lib ad numerú de .xx. in ora .7 xv. sextar mellis.

ABOVE: *A sweetener for the taxman – the people of Leicester (a city that had been part of the Danelaw, with Viking traditions) paid in honey as well as money.*

Crime and punishment

Before 1066, it was noted, if one Welshman killed another, the dead man's relatives could exact retribution on the killer and his family (even burning their houses) until burial of the victim the next day. The king took one third of any plunder from this. Stealing a cow or a woman in Herefordshire meant a fine of 20 shillings after the stolen goods had been returned. A sheep cost less – 2 shillings.

LEFT: *William the Conqueror rides forth with his men at arms; a 14th-century view portrays the ruthless soldier as a chivalrous knight.*

The Domesday Heritage

ABOVE: *A good harvest meant the difference between a healthy winter and the misery of famine. Domesday still mattered to these 14th-century peasants, who may have been working the same land as their 11th-century ancestors.*

The Domesday Book is unique. Through the centuries it has been a symbol to the people of England, who have viewed it – sometimes from completely opposite positions – according to the experience of their age. To the English of 1086, it was a symbol of defeat and oppression – conquest by the pen, as well as by the sword. Yet to peasants of the 1300s it meant hope of an escape from the tied labour demanded by a landlord. Some of those same landlords saw it as enshrining their feudal rights.

Successive ages have treated Domesday with the utmost respect, for it represents a continuity of history that few nations could rival. It has, over the centuries, been used as the basis for investigating rights and titles to land, and has been cited in court cases right through to the 20th century.

To be mentioned in Domesday grants the ultimate historical status to the 13,418 places listed, whether their subsequent fate was to boom and grow, or to stagnate and diminish. Very few vanished altogether – a tribute to the stability of English history. Domesday matters because it determined England's future after William of Normandy's conquest. Drawing a line under the pre-1066 order, it made Norman rule in England 'official' and so provided the foundation on which the new country evolved – in government, bureaucracy and law – from the old.

ABOVE: *Cross-legged on his throne, the king dispenses justice, sceptre in hand. Miscreants hang close by. Lesser breaches of Domesday regulations were dealt with by the lord at his manor court.*

LEFT: *The funeral of William I, who died in 1087, a year after the Domesday survey. He was succeeded as King of England by his son, William II (Rufus), whose coronation is shown on the right of the illustration.*

Slipping away

Then [1066] 2 carucates of land, now 1, the sea has carried off the other … then 12 smallholders, now 2. Then 120 burgesses, now 236.' The good townsfolk of Dunwich in Suffolk paid 60,000 herrings as a gift – Dunwich in 1086 was a prosperous town, and would remain so for another 200 years. But the encroaching sea was unstoppable; first the port was abandoned (1328), then a storm destroyed many houses; and by the 1750s only one church and 35 houses remained. Legend says the bells of the drowned churches still toll beneath the waves.

LEFT: *This 1786 painting by Thomas Hearne shows Saxon stonework on the ruins of the Church of the Hospice of St James, Dunwich.*

What Happened to Domesday?

Domesday stayed with the Royal Treasury at Winchester from the late 11th century onwards, although it also moved about with the royal household from time to time. In the 13th century it went to Westminster in London and there, from King John's reign to Queen Victoria's, was kept in the Treasury of the Receipt of the Exchequer. Until the late 15th century, at least, it was probably stored for safety in Westminster Abbey's Chamber of the Pyx, although it was still taken out and about by the king's treasury officials.

The Book travelled north with Edward II during the wars with the Scots. It went to York in 1300, and to Lincoln. In 1319, 'the clerks of the Exchequer left London for York with twenty-one carts carrying rolls and Domesday Book'. To escape the ravages of the plague during Elizabeth I's reign, it is probable that Exchequer officials took the volumes with them to Hertford. And in September 1666, Domesday must have gone with 'His Majesty's treasure, records and all other things belonging to the said office [Receipt of the Exchequer] from Westminster to Nonsuch [Palace]' after the Great Fire of London.

ABOVE: *A coin of William I, without whom the Domesday Book would almost certainly not have been written.*

By 1631 Domesday was said to be in Tally Court, Westminster, and scholars were studying it as a unique historical source rather than a legal record. 'The book is very ancient and hard to read, and who so findeth anything must pay for the copy of every line 4d ….' From the 17th century it was kept in a stout wooden chest, reinforced with iron straps, and with three locks. The volumes later moved to the Westminster Abbey Chapter House before finding another home in 1859, in the new Public Record Office, Chancery Lane, London.

Fear of bombing in 1918 saw Domesday evacuated to Bodmin Prison in Devon, and in the summer of 1939 it was sent under armed guard to Somerset, to sit out the Second World War in the women's wing of Shepton Mallet Prison. Restored to London in 1945, it now resides with The National Archives at Kew.

RIGHT: *Exeter Cathedral holds Exon Domesday, the return for the south-western circuit, which is valuable for the greater detail it gives of livestock and of named tenants. It has been in the cathedral since at least 1669.*

FAR RIGHT: *Westminster Abbey's Pyx Chamber was originally a chapel, but became the monastery's treasury in the 14th century.*